I0668032

ENDURETH!

A Journal for the Woman Who Knows - Joy Comes

EMILY CLAUDETTE FREEMAN

Endureth! by Emily Claudette Freeman

©November 2015, Emily Claudette Freeman
Graphic Design by Jenette Antonio Sityar

Published by Pecan Tree Publishing, Hollywood, Fl

www.pecantreebooks.com

Library of Congress: 2016931956

ISBN: 978-0-9888969-3-2

PECAN TREE PUBLISHING

Hollywood, Fl.
www.pecantreebooks.com

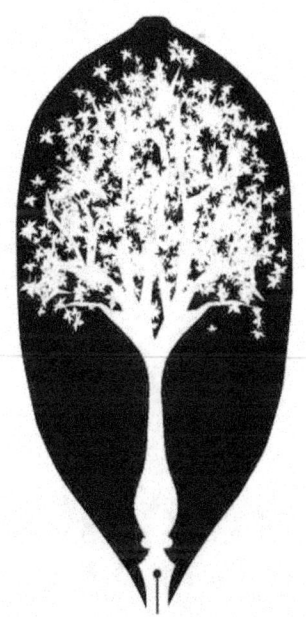

New Voices | New Styles | New Vision

ENDURETH!

A Journal for the Woman Who Knows - Joy Comes

EMILY CLAUDETTE FREEMAN

Welcome Message

Wow! How awesome it is to have you hold this journal in your hands. Endureth!—part of the Enduring Woman Journal Collection is the first journal to be released in a series of planned journal collections. Endureth! is a celebration of and a warm hug for women who have bottled jars and jars of tears, hopes and dreams as they endured and reached for the life they knew and know is their destiny.

Endure—endureth—once seemed like harsh words to me. They rang with—put up with it (whatever it is), be quiet and just do it and other defeating verbiage. Until, I lived the power that comes through enduring. The faith that comes through enduring. The compassion, empathy and understanding that comes through enduring. Yeah! In the endurance—I found The Spirit within. Write your power and endure in joy as you do!

Endureth—my sista—endureth!

Emily Claudette Freeman

ENDURETH!

In the face of pure hell and all its foolishness
In spite of every bad word and ill wish
In the perplexities and seeming certainty
of your doubt
When faith appears a fading dream,
Burdens seem commonplace and life gets to heavy

ENDURETH!

You can still laugh from the depth of your spirit ~ while you cry

I ENDURE Because...

E

$\mathcal{E}$

Exodus 18:23

If thou shalt do this thing, and God command thee so, then thou shalt be able to endure, and all this people shall also go to their place in peace.

I ENDURE Because...

E

E

You can still wipe the tears away and see ahead -
Enduring promises cover you

I ENDURE Because...

E

Psalm 100:5

*For the Lord is good; his mercy is everlasting;
and his truth endureth to all generations.*

I ENDURE Because...

ℰ

E

*Call out to Him - and allow Him to carry you,
rescue you, pick you up*

I ENDURE Because...

E

Psalm 30:5

For his anger endureth but a moment; in his favour is life: weeping may endure for a night, but joy cometh in the morning.

I ENDURE Because...

E

E

You can decide to fight and not to faint ~ You can decide to endure ~ in spite of

I ENDURE Because...

E

Psalm 89:36

His seed shall endure for ever, and his throne as the sun before me.

I ENDURE Because...

$\mathcal{E}$

E

In spite of every bad word and ill wish
~ Endureth

I ENDURE Because...

E

E

When tears spring to the edges of your eyes, yet are too heavy to fall - Endureth

I ENDURE Because...

$\mathcal{E}$

E

Psalm 72:5

They shall fear thee as long as the sun and moon endure, throughout all generations.

I ENDURE Because...

E

E

Endureth - Faith appears, Love appears, Joy appears, Peace appears

I ENDURE Because...

$\mathcal{E}$

E

ℰ

Endure - you can. Endure - you will.
Endure - you did.

I ENDURE Because...

2 Timothy 2:3

Thou therefore endure hardness, as a good soldier of Jesus Christ.

I ENDURE Because...

_E_

E

ENDURETH!
In the face of pure hell and all its foolishness
In spite of every bad word and ill wish
In the perplexities and seeming certainty
of your doubt
When faith appears a fading dream,
Burdens seem commonplace and life gets to heavy

ENDURETH!
When the test pierces you like nothing
You've ever known
And tears spring to the edges of your eyes yet are too heavy to fall,
so they sit in your spirit
And it seems that being forsaken is all that
You can be
But you decide to fight and not to faint, yet you don't know what to
fight

ENDURETH!
When the Father chastises the one He loves
He corrects the one He will raise up
And in that place of parenting, you call out to Him
To carry you, rescue you, pick you up
And wrap you up

ENDURETH!
Because you didn't just exhale - you inhaled too
Because you can still laugh from the depth of your spirit - while you
cry
Because you can live for your destiny and live for your self
and because, MY LORD – MY LORD,
You can still wipe the tears away and see ahead
and above

ENDURETH!

Journals in the Keepsake Power Series:

Powerfully Peculiar
Be Made Whole
Wonderfully Made and Wonderfully God's

Journals in the Enduring Woman Series:

Every Woman In You Should_____!
Endureth!
Unlayered and Free

For Individual Orders, visit us at: www.pecantreebooks.com.

For Bulk Orders, email us at: info@pecantreebooks.com

For literary and spiritual empowerment workshops,
contact E. Claudette Freeman, at: coaching@eclaudetteliterary.com or
visit the website, www.eclaudetteliterary.com.

www.ingramcontent.com/pod-product-compliance
Lightning Source LLC
Chambersburg PA
CBHW051511260626
47162CB00008B/2922